DATE

WITHDRAWN

Be Smart About Your Career

COLLEGE, INCOME, AND CAREERS

Amy Graham

BE SMART
ABOUT
MONEY
AND
FINANCIAL
LITERACY

CAREER
☑ Advancement Potential
☑ Making a Difference
☑ Enjoyable Work

Enslow Publishers, Inc.
40 Industrial Road
Box 398
Berkeley Heights, NJ 07922
USA

http://www.enslow.com

Library of Congress Cataloging-in-Publication Data

Graham, Amy.
  Be smart about your career : college, income, and careers / Amy Graham.
    pages cm. — (Be smart about money and financial literacy)
  Includes index.
  Summary: "Examines college, income, and careers, including choosing the best post-secondary option and paying for college; identifying career interests, setting career goals, and planning how to achieve them; and understanding income, both earned and unearned"—Provided by publisher.
  Audience: Grade 9 to 12
  ISBN 978-0-7660-4286-5
  1. Vocational guidance. 2. Career development—Juvenile literature.
  3. High school graduates—Employment—Juvenile literature. 4. Finance, Personal—Juvenile literature. I. Title.
  HF5381.2.G73 2013
   650.1—dc23

                              2013006488

Future editions:
Paperback ISBN: 978-1-4644-0521-1
EPUB ISBN: 978-1-4645-1266-7
Single-User PDF ISBN: 978-1-4646-1266-4
Multi-User PDF ISBN: 978-0-7660-5898-9

Printed in the United States of America
112013 Bang Printing, Brainerd, Minn.
10 9 8 7 6 5 4 3 2 1

To Our Readers: We have done our best to make sure all Internet addresses in this book were active and appropriate when we went to press. However, the author and the publisher have no control over and assume no liability for the material available on those Internet sites or on other Web sites they may link to. Any comments or suggestions can be sent by e-mail to comments@enslow.com or to the address on the back cover.

Illustration Credits: Shutterstock.com

Cover Illustration: Shutterstock.com (George Washington) and © iStockphoto.com / Amanda Rohde (colonial suit).

Contents

Throughout the book, look for this logo 😊 for smart financial tips and this logo 😠 for bad choices to avoid. Also, don't forget to "Do the Math" at the end of each chapter.

Living Your Dream

Chapter 1

If you could have any job in the world—any job at all—what would you do?

Forget about any obstacles that might stand in your way. Your ideal job would make you feel happy, fulfilled, and excited to start your day. Go ahead, close your eyes, just for a few minutes, and see what you come up with.

So . . . what did you picture yourself doing?

Some people know right away what they would do. Maybe you have known you wanted to be a veterinarian since you were six. If you are one of those people, congratulations! You are well on your path to living your dream.

What if you were not able to come up with . . . well, anything? Hey, don't feel bad. Most students have no idea what they want to do. Part of the problem is that, as a student, you have a limited idea of what jobs are available. Sure, you know about your parents' jobs. You have seen your teachers, your doctor, your dentist, and other people in your community at work. Then there are the jobs portrayed on television and in the movies. How many job openings are there for rock stars and rogue detectives, anyway? In truth, there are a myriad of opportunities for you to choose from, including many jobs you have never even heard of.

Job or Career

What is the difference between a job and a career? We often use these words interchangeably, but they have distinct meanings. A job is a piece of work that you get paid for. You can take a job baby-sitting for an evening, or you can get a job washing dishes in a restaurant. You earn money and work gets done.

A career, on the other hand, is a profession or occupation that you pursue as your life's work. For example, let's look at a student who likes to work with children. She takes a job after high school working with preschool children in a day-care center. To advance her career, she attends a four-year college for a degree in elementary school education and is able to get a job as a teacher. After years of teaching, she pursues a master's degree in school administration and becomes a principal. Over the course of her career in education, she keeps learning new skills, which allow her to get jobs that pay better.

When it comes time for you to pick a career, how will you decide what to do? First of all, don't worry. You don't have to decide what to do right now. No one expects you to have all the answers by the end of high school or college. Even when you enter the workforce, it takes time to figure out the right career for you. People rarely find the perfect career immediately. In a July 2012 study by the Bureau of Labor Statistics, Americans held an average of eleven different jobs between the ages of eighteen and forty-four. Almost half of these job changes occurred before the age of twenty-four.

Your career path is a journey. The road will twist and turn as you learn new skills and try out new opportunities. But the fact remains that you will never get your dream job if you do not stop to identify what your dream job might be. It will pay off if you take some time, do some research, and give your future some serious consideration.

Identify Your Interests and Skills

The first step in deciding what you would like to do is to identify what you are passionate about. "Choose a job you love and you will never have to work a day in your life." This wise quote is attributed to Confucius, an ancient Chinese philosopher. There are thousands of different jobs you can do, so why not do one that you truly enjoy? Identify what it is you like to do. Pay attention to what makes you happy. What do people tell you that you are good at? What do you get most excited talking about? What are your talents or skills?

Most importantly, try new things that look interesting. Don't wait for opportunities to cross your path—seek them out! You may not have encountered anything you feel enthusiastic about yet.

New experiences open up possibilities. Bad or good, new experiences keep us learning. The ability to learn new skills is a vital part of having a successful career. When you find something that interests you, learn as much as you can about it.

Talk to your friends and family—people you trust—about what they see as your interests, values, and talents. Surround yourself with people who support and believe in you. Listen to your inner voice first and foremost. Your ideas about a perfect job may change during your life, but your core values and strengths will remain the same. It is never too early to identify what you enjoy. When you have ideas, write them down. Revisit your ideas in a few weeks or a few months. Do they still hold true? Add new ideas as you think of them.

Identify one thing that you feel passionate about. Visit the Bureau of Labor Statistics (<www.bls.gov/k12/>) and research the job possibilities in your field of interest.

Assume a job will be waiting for you when you graduate from high school.

Now it's your turn to "Do the Math." The end of each chapter features a math or word problem. Use what you learned in the chapter to help you answer the questions. The right math will help you make the right financial decisions.

Do the Math

Brainstorming Exercise
Circle the words that describe you:

Creative, Bold, Analytical, Thoughtful, Calm, Dramatic, Problem Solver, Kind, Helpful, Talkative, Inventive, Tactful, Mechanically Inclined, Caring, Good With Technology, Encouraging, Musical, Enjoy Debating, Political, Good at Working With Your Hands, Enjoy Spending Time Outside, Good at Fixing Things, Animal Lover, Patient, Focused, Strong Writing Skills, Good at Listening, Like to Organize Data, Observant, Compassionate, Curious, Levelheaded, Like to Work With Children, Like to Work With the Elderly, Thrill Seeking, Physically Active, Interested in Medical Sciences, Articulate, Adventurous, Discreet, Fair, Interested in Health, Persuasive, Calm in An Emergency.

Circle the jobs that sound interesting to you:

Journalist, Elementary Schoolteacher, Veterinarian, Photographer, Farmer, Social Worker, Lawyer, Dentist, Optometrist (Eye Doctor), Surgeon, Architect, Airline

Pilot, Marine, Graphic Designer, Civil Engineer, Landscape Architect, Construction Worker, Electrician, Forester, Computer Programmer, Software Developer, Health Educator, Accountant, Real Estate Broker, Financial Analyst, Dancer, Librarian, Actor, Professional Athlete, Mathematician, Entrepreneur, Fitness Trainer, Archaeologist, Meteorologist, Historian, Chemist, Wildlife Biologist, Astronomer, Psychologist, College Professor, Registered Nurse, Massage Therapist, Nutritionist, Pharmacist, Respiratory Therapist, Pediatrician, Physician, Translator, Broadcast News Analyst, Film Editor, Camera Operator, Bank Teller, Police Dispatcher, Aircraft Mechanic, Appliance Repairer, Small Engine Mechanic, Desktop Publisher, Musician, Legislator, High School Principal, Business Executive, Insurance Sales Agent, Firefighter, Police Officer.

Do the words you circled to describe you relate to the jobs that sound interesting to you? How will those traits you circled help you in that career?

Money Makes the World Go 'Round

Wait, what's this about money? What happened to connecting with your passion and pursuing your dreams? Where does money fit in? Everybody knows that "money can't buy happiness." But it is time for a reality check, people. Like it or not, money is a fact of life. It is a piece of the puzzle you will need to think about when you embark on your career path.

Money Means Choices

The career you choose will determine your income, or the amount of money you earn. Your income will determine what kind of lifestyle you can afford. The more money you earn, the more choices you will have. In other words, your career will control how much money you can spend. Maybe that seems obvious, but it is an important point in terms of day-to-day decision making.

Your income will determine whether you can buy a car or have to take the bus to work. It will affect whether you shop for clothes at an upscale boutique or at a thrift shop. It will decide whether you go out with friends on the weekend or stay at home with the cat. Should money be the most important factor in deciding what you want to do? No. Do you need to consider it, even if you do not consider money to be important? Yes, emphatically, yes. Having money means you can make choices.

Living Wage

How much money will you need? It can be hard to envision. You may not have a clear idea of what your basic needs cost. Actually, you may not have a clear idea of what your basic expenses will even BE. What sort of things will you have to pay for when you live on your own? Common expenses include food, housing, health care, and transportation. Utilities—a catch-all category for things like electricity, water, heat, cable, and Internet access—are another expense that can add up fast. You'll also want to put money aside for emergencies and to save up for big-ticket items. So what does all that cost?

According to a 2012 article in *USA Today*, an American family needs an annual income of more than $150,000 to live comfortably. Some families live comfortably on less than that and a few require more. It all depends on your values and how you define living comfortably. Where you choose to live can make a big difference.

Money = Happy?

It turns out money CAN buy happiness, at least up to a point. According to a 2010 study by researchers at Princeton University, people with higher household incomes reported being happier on a daily basis than those with lower incomes. However, at around $75,000, the effects of a higher income on happiness dropped off. If having  plenty of money is important to you, you will want to pick a career that pays well. If your goal is to be happy in life, you will need to think about more than how much money you can earn. You will also need to factor in job satisfaction.

In order to be happy at work, you need to find a job that is a good fit for you. Would you like to work outside or inside, seated at a desk? Do you like to interact with people, or do you prefer to work independently? Do you like to be in the public eye or behind the scenes? Are you willing to work long hours, or is your free time important?

There are self-assessment tools to help you figure out what kind of work suits you. Unlike most tests, there is no pass or fail grade and the results can be enlightening. Your school counselor or a job counselor can help you find self-assessment tools.

But I Don't Have Any Money

So what? Not many students have money. You can seek out opportunities to learn new skills no matter what your current financial situation. Don't let a lack of money stop you from pursuing a rewarding career. This might inspire you: Successful business owners are more likely to start out poor than rich.

Once you have identified your career goal, you need to come up with a plan for how you can achieve it. What education or training do you need to be qualified for your dream job? How can you get those skills? Do some research. The U.S. Bureau of Labor Statistics publishes *The Occupational Outlook Handbook* each year. The handbook which is available for free online—is a great place to learn more about jobs you are interested in. It describes what kind of education is needed for a job, how many jobs there are in the United States, and predicts how the job market will grow in the future.

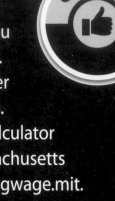

Have an idea of how much money you will need to earn to live comfortably. Consider whether your chosen career will pay enough to cover your needs. Check out this online living wage calculator developed by scientists at the Massachusetts Institute of Technology: <http://livingwage.mit.edu/>. By entering your city or town, you can see how much money an individual needs to live in your area.

Some bad ways to pick a career or job:

- To make your parents or someone else happy.

- To impress your friends because it seems like a cool thing to do.

- To get a paycheck as soon as possible.

- Because someone once said they thought you'd be good at it.

Do the Math

● Dylan graduated college with a four-year bachelor's degree in journalism. He has a job writing for a popular online newspaper and has a take-home pay of $560 a week.

● Annie has a master's degree in microbiology. She works as a lab researcher at a university and brings home a paycheck for $950 a week.

● Elise has not gone to college. She has a job as a customer service representative at a catalog company. Her paycheck is for $375 a week.

● Dylan, Annie, and Elise each work 40 hours per week.

They each spend $125 a week on food. How many hours would each of them have to work to afford his or her weekly grocery bill?

College: Investing in Your Future

Chapter 3

Why go to college? Why not start earning a paycheck as soon as you get that high school diploma? After all, the sooner you get a job, the sooner you can start putting money in the bank, right? The answer is simple: The more education you have, the more money you can earn—and not just a little more money but a lot more money. According to the U.S. Census Bureau, over the course of a lifetime, a college graduate can earn over a million dollars more than a high school graduate.

That does not mean you can't earn a decent living if you don't go to college. With determination and the right set of skills, anybody can have a successful career. However, education will open doors for you. College graduates have higher on average earnings than workers who do not earn a college degree. College graduates are able to land better jobs. They are less likely to lose their jobs during an economic downturn. There are many ways you can use education to get started on your career path.

Education Pays		
Unemployment rate in 2012 (in%)		Median weekly earnings in 2012 (in$)
2.5	Doctoral degree	1,624
2.1	Professional degree	1,735
3.5	Master's degree	1,300
4.5	Bachelor's degree	1,066
6.2	Associate's degree	785
7.7	Some college, no degree	727
8.3	High school diploma	652
12.4	Less than high school diploma	471
Average: 6.8%		Average: $815

Source: Bureau of Labor Statistics, Current Population Survey

Postsecondary Nondegree Awards

You don't have to go to a four-year college to advance your career. Some careers only require a postsecondary award and some on-the-job training. Don't let the word postsecondary intimidate you—it is just another way of saying "after high school." How long does it take to earn one of these? The amount of training can

vary widely, depending on what you study. They can take anywhere from a few weeks to a few years to achieve.

What kind of careers are we talking about here? These are jobs for firefighters, emergency medical technicians, and electronics repairers. For example, in 2010, an aircraft mechanic made an average annual salary of $53,420. This job requires a postsecondary award that can be obtained within 18–24 months. A commercial pilot's median salary was $67,500. A commercial pilot must have a pilot's license, which requires 250 hours of flight experience, as well as undergoing on-the-job training. Getting a postsecondary nondegree award can be a smart and affordable way to kick off your career.

Associate's Degree

It takes about two years to earn an associate's degree. You can pursue one of these degrees at a community college. What's the difference between a community college and a four-year college? A community college is typically smaller and less expensive than a four-year college. There is often no option to live on campus. Some students can't attend school full-time. They need to juggle school with work or family. Community college can be a good choice for them. These schools excel at preparing people for jobs that are in high demand.

With an associate's degree, you can qualify for a job in the fast-growing field of health care. You can study to become a registered nurse (median annual salary $64,690), a medical transcriptionist ($39,200 median salary), or a physical therapy aide ($37,710 median salary)—just to name a few options. Other jobs that can be acquired with an associate's degree are bookkeeper, paralegal, and mechanic. Community college students can also choose to transfer their credits to a four-year college. Some students want to go to a four-year college but did not earn high enough grades in high school to get accepted at a four-year institution. This is a good way to bring up their grades and prove they are serious about their education.

Bachelor's Degree

When people say they plan to go to college after high school, they usually mean they are going to a four-year college. This is where you can earn a bachelor's degree in the arts (BA) or in the sciences (BS). A four-year degree gives you the skills you need to do many jobs, such as computer programmer ($71,380 median salary), teacher ($53,230 median salary), graphic designer ($43,500 median salary), mechanical engineer ($78,160 median salary), or social worker ($42,480 median salary).

Colleges come in a wide variety, from tiny liberal arts colleges to huge research universities. State colleges and universities are public schools. The government helps to fund them. For the most part, they don't cost as much as a private college or university does.

What's the difference between a college and a university? That is tricky. Often the two terms are used interchangeably. A university offers opportunities to study beyond a bachelor's degree.

Master's and Professional Degrees

Master's degrees and doctoral degrees require more than four years of college. On the downside, it is a big investment of both time and money. On the upside, you are then highly qualified for some of the best-paying jobs in the nation. Architects ($72,550 median salary), college professors ($62,050 median salary), physicians and surgeons ($166,440 median salary), dentists ($146,920 median salary), lawyers ($112,760 median salary), and veterinarians ($82,040 median salary) are all professions that require a master's or professional degree.

High Wages Without the Degree

Traditional advice is that you need at least a bachelor's degree to land a high-paying job.

This is not true, according to the Bureau of Labor Statistics. There are more than eighty professions with average salaries of more than $50,000 per year that do not require a four-year degree. These include air-traffic controllers, who have an average annual salary of $108,040.

Often these well-paying jobs require working long hours under a high level of stress or danger. There are many job openings in the field of medicine and health that fall into this category. For example, emergency room nurses often work long twelve-hour shifts helping people in medical emergencies. Their ability to act quickly and efficiently can be the difference between life and death. Radiation and sonogram technicians, respiratory therapists, and occupational therapy assistants are other well-paying positions in high demand that do not require a four-year degree.

Some smart ways to pick colleges to apply for:

- Because it has a strong department in your area of interest. *If you know what field you want to study, this is the number one reason to choose a school.*

- Because you have visited the college and had a positive experience. *While this shouldn't be your only reason, you should make it a priority to visit the schools you consider attending.*

- Because it has been personally recommended to you by someone in your chosen career field. *Personal experience in turning a college degree into a rewarding career? You've got to pay attention to that!*

- Because it offers a wide range of interesting courses in your intended major. *College is your chance to learn all you can about your field of interest—you want to make the most of it.*

- Because it would expose you to some amazing opportunities that you couldn't get somewhere else. *Semester abroad to Japan? Marine program in the Galapagos Islands? Archaeology in Israel?*

Be Smart About Your Career

Some bad ways to choose which colleges to apply to:

- Because your friends are going there. *Trust me: Wherever you go, you will make new friends at college. You can stay in touch with your high school friends without tagging along with them.*

- Because it is an elite school and you want to impress people. *Apply to a school you have a chance at getting into, not to impress people.*

- Because it has winning sports teams. *Unless you're getting a scholarship to play for that winning sports team, not a good choice.*

- Because it is a family tradition. *Just because it was your parent's alma mater doesn't mean it is a good fit for you.*

- Because it is an inexpensive school. *Once you take into account scholarships and grants, a more expensive college might end up costing you less. Don't rule out a school you are interested in based on cost until you get the financial aid package.*

College: Investing in Your Future

Do the Math

Education Pays		
Unemployment rate in 2012 (in%)		Median weekly earnings in 2012 (in$)
2.5	Doctoral degree	1,624
2.1	Professional degree	1,735
3.5	Master's degree	1,300
4.5	Bachelor's degree	1,066
6.2	Associate's degree	785
7.7	Some college, no degree	727
8.3	High school diploma	652
12.4	Less than high school diploma	471
Average: 6.8%		Average: $815

Source: Bureau of Labor Statistics, Current Population Survey

1. Using the data from this chart (also shown on page 19), determine the median annual earnings for each educational level.
2. What is the difference between the median earnings of a worker with a professional degree and the median workings of a worker with a high school diploma over a twenty-five year career?

Be Smart About Your Career

How Will I Pay for College?

We've established that college is a good way to gain the skills and education necessary to launch your career. A postsecondary award or degree is the key to making a decent income. It will give you choices about how to live your life. But how will you pay for school?

College tuition is not cheap. The price of college is climbing steadily every year. CNN reported that for the 2012–2013 school year, it costs an average of $22,261 to go to an in-state public college. Maybe you think that price tag covers your entire college experience? No, that is the cost for just one year. It costs nearly twice as much to attend a private college. Let's assume that you, like most people, do not have hundreds of thousands in the bank. How will you pay for college?

Some students are fortunate enough to have parents or grandparents who have set aside money to help pay for their education. A college generally expects parents to pay for a portion of their child's tuition, though not all parents are able or willing to help. If your family doesn't have that kind of money, don't despair. The federal government offers more than 150 billion dollars in financial aid funding for students each year. Two thirds of all college students receive financial aid from the federal government. Other financial aid is available at the state level.

When you are accepted at a college, you receive a financial aid package. This documents how much your college will cost and how much your family will need to pay. It lists any scholarships, grants, loans, or work-study jobs that will help you come up with the funds you need to attend school.

Free Money for College

Grants and scholarships are money for college that you do not need to pay back. It's free money! Colleges give grants to students who can demonstrate they have a financial need. A scholarship is money that colleges use to attract the best students. If your grades are top notch or if you excel at a sport, a college may offer you a partial scholarship for the privilege of having you attend. Occasionally, schools are able to offer a student a full scholarship— one that covers the cost of the entire tuition. Scholarships can be offered on merit or financial need. One thing to know: Usually, scholarships depend on your school performance. They can be taken away if you do not keep your grades up.

Cast a wide net for grants and scholarships, because it's not just colleges that give them out. Some organizations, for example the American Legion and the Elks Club, give out scholarships to the children of their members. Other groups, like the American Medical Association, provide scholarships to support students who are going into their field.

Student Loans

A student loan is money for college, but it is not free. Students agree to pay back the money, with interest, after they graduate. Interest is money you pay in addition to the amount of the money you borrow. How much interest you owe depends on the interest rate. The higher the interest rate, the more money you will owe.

You do not have to pay back the loan immediately after graduating. Usually, there is a grace period of at least six months before you start making monthly payments. This allows you time to find work using your new skills and start earning money. A typical loan has a term of up to ten years—meaning you will be making monthly payments for ten years.

The best source of loans for students is the U.S. Department of Education. Parents are also eligible for federal loans to help pay for their child's education. Private institutions offer alternative educational loans to both students and their parents. These should be your last choice to fund your education. The terms of these loans are never as good as federal loans. The interest rates are often much higher and can be downright predatory. If you're not careful, you can end up with more debt than you can pay back.

Plan Ahead

Even if you receive financial aid, you're probably going to have to chip in from your own pocket. If you don't have a college fund already set up, go ahead and start one. It is never too late to start saving for college. Many students take jobs in high school and during summer vacation to save money for college. The more you can pay up front, the less debt you will have when you graduate. If you pursue an advanced degree, you will be in a position to earn more money after school to pay back your student loans.

The ugly truth is that in today's economy, a college degree does not guarantee a good job after you graduate. The Associated Press reported in April 2012 that half of new college graduates were either without a job or underemployed. To be underemployed means you are working at a job that does not make use, or meet the qualifications, of your skills and training. When a college graduate takes a job bagging groceries, he is underemployed.

What happens when a student graduates from college with debt and is unable to get a job? An increasing number of graduates face this problem. Student debt is a serious problem in the United States. It now exceeds one trillion dollars.

According to *Businessweek*, student loan defaults were at a fourteen-year high in 2012. When a person defaults on a student loan, it means she fails to repay the money she has borrowed to pay for her college education. It is more important than ever to think carefully about how you will pay for college. If you can graduate with little to no debt, you will be in an excellent position to begin your career. When you land your first job out of college, you'll be able to use your income to begin building your wealth. It is okay to borrow money for school, but not more than you can pay back.

You cannot receive money for school unless you take the time to apply for it. After January 1st of your senior year of high school, fill out the Free Application for Federal Student Aid (FAFSA) at <www.fafsa.ed.gov>. After you fill out the FAFSA, you will receive your EFC, or Expected Family Contribution. This is the magic number that helps schools and states determine how much aid you need. No matter what your financial situation, you should fill out the FAFSA. It is the only way to learn what student aid you are eligible for.

Decide on a school before you fully understand the financial aid package. You need to know if you can afford the tuition and how you will pay for it before you commit.

Do the Math

Jake is trying to decide between two colleges. He is interested in computer programming and both colleges have excellent programs. He has some savings from his part-time job ($3,000) he plans to use toward his college tuition and expenses. His parents are able to contribute $1,200 per school year.

The first college costs $20,105 a year. They are offering Jake a $5,000 grant, a $3,200 scholarship, an on-campus work-study job earning $3,600, and a $4,875 student loan.

The second college costs $22,800 a year. They have offered Jake $13,500 student loan package, a $5,000 grant, and $2,900 on campus work-study job.

Financially, which college makes the most sense for Jake? Why?

Understanding Income

When it comes time to support yourself as an adult, you'll need an income. Most people get their income through wages. The money you earn when you work at a job is your wage. We call it earned income because you work for it. The downside to earned income is that once you stop working, you stop making money. In order to earn more money, you must work more hours or learn a new skill that allows you to earn more per hour. Another type of income is unearned income: We will talk more about unearned income later. First, let's take a look at earned income.

Your Paycheck

When you get a job, you and your employer agree on either an hourly wage or annual salary. An hourly wage is how much you will be paid for each hour you work. An annual salary is how much you will be paid each year. Most employers pay their employees at the end of every week or bimonthly (twice a month). Along with your paycheck, you will receive an income statement that details how much you earned and your withholdings.

Withholdings can come as a shock to first-time wage earners. Here is the bad news. You worked forty hours and earned ten dollars an hour, but your paycheck will be less than $400. Wait—what? If you earn twenty dollars to mow the lawn at home, you are get a $20 bill after you mow the lawn. When you work for an employer, some of your earnings are set aside—or withheld—each pay period. This money pays for federal and state taxes, Social Security, and Medicare.

Federal and State Taxes

A tax is money that your government demands from you. The government levies taxes on things such as income, property, and sales. Complain if you will, but the price of living in a civilized nation is to pay taxes. Workers pay income taxes to the state as well as to the federal government. Governments use taxes to pay for all sorts of things that we depend on, such as police and fire departments, roads, schools, and libraries. The government sets aside some of each of your paychecks. That way, when your income tax is due on April 15 each year, you are not scrambling to come up with the money.

When you begin your employment, your employer will ask you to fill out a W-4 tax form required by the Internal Revenue

Service (IRS). On the form, there is a place to claim exemptions. This is how your employer determines how much tax to withhold from your pay. The more exemptions you claim, the bigger your paycheck will be. If you claim fewer exemptions, your paycheck will be smaller. However, you will not have to come up with as much money at tax time. In fact, you may even receive a tax refund when you file your taxes. You will probably claim an exemption of zero (if you are still dependent on your parents) or one when you fill out your first W-4 form.

Social Security

This is a government retirement program for workers and their families. It also helps people who are unable to work because of a long-term disability. Workers and their employers pay money into the Social Security system. This money earns interest over the years. When the worker retires or can no longer work due to a disability, she receives a monthly payment from the Social Security trust fund. The Social Security program began in 1937. It was part of President Franklin D. Roosevelt's plan to help America recover from the Great Depression.

Medicare

Medicare is a government-sponsored health insurance for seniors. Workers pay money into the Medicare system while they are in the workforce. When a worker reaches the age of sixty-five, he receives medical insurance coverage through Medicare.

Employee Benefits

Employers often offer incentives in addition to wages. These are called employee benefits. A common benefit is paid vacation days. This allows you to take days off from work and still be paid. Health and dental insurance, paid sick time, gym membership, medical reimbursement accounts, and company discounts are other forms of employee benefits. When you consider a job offer, you will want to factor in the value of any benefits. They can be worth thousands of dollars each year!

Unearned Income

So we have determined that most people make money through earned income. But what about unearned income? Unearned income is any kind of money you receive that you did not have to work for. Think about the $20 bill that your grandmother slips into your birthday card. Gifts, inheritances, lottery winnings—these are all types of unearned income. Unearned income also includes money you get when you invest. Imagine having an income that is not tied to the hours that you work. Save your money, invest it wisely, and you can reap the benefits of unearned income.

Remember when we talked about interest in Chapter 4? When you borrow money for school in the form of a loan, you pay interest. That interest can really add up. You want to get as low an interest rate as possible when you have to take out a loan. But interest can work for you, too. One form of unearned income is interest.

When you invest your money, you can be the one earning the interest. Visit <http://www.themint.org/tweens/compounding-calculator2.html> to learn more about how you can put your money to work for you!

Here's a mistake to avoid: Don't make a budget based on your gross pay. Your gross pay is the amount you are paid before taxes and other withholdings have been taken out. It can be much higher than your net pay, which is the amount of your paycheck. Visit www.paycheckcity.com to use their free paycheck calculator. Experiment by changing the amount of your withholdings. You can see how this affects the amount of your paycheck.

Do the Math

123 - John R. Doe				Required Deductions		

Pay Period 06/07/13 to 06/21/13

Earnings				Federal Income Tax	00.00	00.00
				FICA - Medicare	06.08	12.16
Hours	**Rate**	**This Period**	**YTD**	WI State Income Tax	00.00	00.00
50	9.00	450.00	900.00	FICA - Social Security	25.92	51.84
				Other Deductions		
				Health Insurance	00.00	00.00
Gross Pay		**450.00**	**900.00**	401k	00.00	00.00
				Parking	00.00	00.00
				NET PAY	**418.00**	**836.00**

Your Employer   Check Number: XXXXXX
1234 Some Street   Pay Date: 06/24/13
Milwaukee, WI ZIP CODE

PAY   ***Four hundred eighteen dollars and 00 cents************************$418.00

To the Order of
        John R. Doe
        555 Some Street
        Milwaukee, WI ZIP CODE

1. The image above is a mock paycheck. Answer the following questions by using the paycheck:
     A. How much is the employee paid per hour?
     B. How much federal tax is withheld?
     C. How much social security is withheld this pay period?
     D. How much Medicare is withheld this pay period?
     E. How much less is the net pay than the gross pay for the period?
2. Thad earns $18.50 an hour at his current job. Another company has offered him a position making $40,000 a year for the same type of work. The new position would have similar benefits, with one major difference. It would not include health insurance. His current job covers his health insurance premium—a monthly cost of $600. Does it make sense for him to take the new job or would he be better off staying in his current job?

Be Smart About Your Career

Take It Further: Be an Entrepreneur

Chapter 6

Entrepreneur: It's an English word that came to us from the French language. It can be hard to say and even harder to spell. But forget all that: What does it mean?

The U.S. Small Business Administration states it well when it says: "An entrepreneur: Sees an opportunity. Makes a plan. Starts the business. Manages the business. Receives the profits." Have you ever dreamed of starting your own business someday? Then you may have what it takes to become an entrepreneur.

Think you need a lot of money to start up a business? Not necessarily. Chris Guillebeau published a book in 2012, *$100 Startup*, in which he interviewed hundreds of successful business owners. His conclusion: You don't need to have a business

degree and attract wealthy investors to make a profit as an entrepreneur. With an innovative idea and dedication, you can start a business for as little as one hundred dollars. He says it is as simple as finding the place where your expertise overlaps with what people are willing to pay for.

What are some reasons to start your own business?

- You want to be your own boss.
- You want the freedom to make creative decisions.
- You want to use your skills to the fullest.
- You want to achieve financial independence.
- You want to pursue something meaningful.

To start a business, you need to write a business plan. A business plan lays out what you want to accomplish and how you will get there. Then you will need to figure out how you will finance your business. Small business owners may take out a loan from a bank or the government, apply for grant money, or find seed money from an investor. You can learn more about starting a business by visiting the U.S. Small Business Administration at their website.

Imagine doing what you love to do and getting paid well for it. This is what motivates entrepreneurs to strike out on their own and take a risk. It may not be for everybody. An entrepreneur needs to be comfortable taking risks. A successful entrepreneur must be self-motivated. She must be innovative and see opportunities where others do not.

Do you like the idea of entrepreneurship but lack a good idea? Let's look at where people get their ideas for starting a business.

- From their hobbies and interests
- From their school or work experience
- From family or friends
- From problems they see in the world around them
- From brainstorming and research

Here are some scenarios of how interests and skills can turn into business ideas. Read these over and then brainstorm your own ideas.

- You love dogs. Wish you could get paid to throw frisbees with Fido in the park? Some people share your love but are too busy to properly care for their dogs. Start a dog-walking or dog-grooming service.
- You love to bake and pies are your specialty. Your family and friends tell you how delicious your pies are. Working parents like to serve homemade pies for holidays but are too busy to bake them. Take orders from your friends' parents for pies during the holidays.
- When it comes to your iPhone, you're an expert. Some people (think grandpa and grandma here) have an iPhone but not the tech savvy to understand how to use it. Offer to train people who want to learn. Earn money by sharing your knowledge with others.

Take It Further: Be an Entrepreneur

It's Your Choice

Whatever you decide to do after high school, remember it's your life. What you choose to do is up to you. These are some important ideas to remember in finding your career path:

- Identify what it is you like to do.
- Learn new skills that build on your interests.
- Research jobs in your field of interest.
- Set a career goal.
- Determine what education and training you will need.
- Make a plan to reach your goal.
- Step-by-step, pursue the education and training you need.

If you want to impress anyone—from a college admissions officer to a future employer—show them that you have a career goal. Talk with them about your plan to reach your goal. Ask for their advice. Most importantly, and please pay attention here—give yourself a chance. You can have a successful career and the lifestyle you choose. Here's what you'll need: a goal, a plan, dedication, hard work, and the belief that you can do it.

You might excel at entrepreneurship if:

- You are a natural leader.

- You like to solve problems.

- You can make plans, set goals, and follow through.

- You like the idea of reaping the benefit of hard work.

- You don't mind working long hours.

- You like to compete with others.

- You are well organized.

You might make a BAD entrepreneur if:

- You'd rather not be the one in charge.

- You tend to procrastinate.

- When you see a problem, your first thought is to blame it on someone else.

- You want to work Monday through Friday 9–5 and enjoy your weekends off.

- You'd rather not work extra unless you have to. It takes a lot to motivate you.

- You have a hard time setting goals, nevermind meeting them.

Take It Further: Be an Entrepreneur

Do the Math

Summer break is starting soon and Jane has set a goal to save $2,000 in her college fund this summer. She'd also like to earn a little extra for spending money. She likes working with children and being her own boss. Look over Jane's work plan below. Can she make enough to reach her goals? List a few ideas of how Jane could increase her earnings.

- Jane makes $8 an hour baby-sitting for a family down the street. They would like to hire her to baby-sit their children for three hours on Tuesday and Thursday afternoons for ten weeks. She can also count on baby-sitting for them a few weekend evenings. She usually earns $40 when she baby-sits on the weekend.

- Last summer Jane helped to run a recreation program for kids in her town. She earned $200 a week for four weeks in July working Monday–Friday mornings. She plans to do this again this summer. She could advertise her baby-sitting services there. She did that last summer and met a lot of families looking for baby-sitting help.

- Jane and her sister have a plan to organize a neighborhood yard sale in their yard during the town's annual summer festival in July. They will advertise by making posters and hanging them up around town. In return, they will charge $10 for neighbors and friends to set up a table. The girls will also have a bake sale table at the event. They hope to earn anywhere from $200–$400.

- Her friend's family is going away to visit their grandmother for the month of August. They've asked Jane if she would water their plants, bring in the mail, and feed their pet fish while they're gone. In return, they'd pay her $100.

Be Smart About Your Career

Glossary

bachelor's degree—A four-year college degree in the arts or sciences.

benefits—Things that employers offer their employees in addition to wages, for example, health insurance and paid vacation days.

budget—An estimate of income and money being spent over a period of time.

debt—Money owed.

default—Failure to pay back money owed.

employee—A worker who works for another person in exchange for money.

employer—A person or business that pays one or more people to do a job.

entrepreneur—A person who creates his or her own business.

exemption—An amount a taxpayer can deduct from the taxes he owes because of age or family status.

grant—Money awarded to students for school that does not need to be paid back.

income—Money received, either for work or from investments.

interest—Charge or fee for the privilege of borrowing money.

job satisfaction—How content you are with your job.

master's degree—A degree for work completed at a higher level than a bachelor's degree.

medical reimbursement account—A job benefit that sets aside some of your salary—without taking out taxes—for medical, dental, and vision expenses that aren't covered by insurance.

Medicare—Government-sponsored health care insurance for seniors.

payroll deductions—Money that is withheld from your paycheck.

postsecondary—After the completion of high school.

salary—Annual amount of money earned for a job you do.

scholarship—Free money for school for students with excellent grades or sports skills.

social security—A government-sponsored retirement program.

student loan—Money for school that must be paid back, with interest.

taxes—Money the government levies on things like income, property, and sales.

wage—Money earned for doing a job.

Learn More

Books

Bolles, Richard with Carol Christen and Jean M. Blomquist. *What Color is Your Parachute? for Teens, 2nd ed.* New York: Ten Speed Press, 2010.

Chany, Kalman. *Paying for College Without Going Broke, 2013 edition.* Princeton, N.J.: Princeton Review, 2012.

Lore, Nicholas. *Now What? The Young Person's Guide to Choosing the Perfect Career.* New York: Simon & Schuster, 2008.

Silivanch, Annalise. *Making the Right College Choice: Technical, 2-Year, 4-Year.* New York: Rosen Publishing Group, 2010.

Internet Addresses

BizKids for Young Entrepreneurs and Students
<http://bizkids.com/students>

College Portrait of Undergraduate Information
<www.collegeportraits.org>

Exploring Career Information From the Bureau of Labor Statistics
<http://www.bls.gov/k12/index.htm>

Do the Math Answer Key

Chapter 1: Living Your Dream
Answers will vary.

Chapter 2: Money Makes the World Go 'Round
First, determine how much each person makes per hour. Divide his or her weekly salary by 40 hours per week.

Dylan makes 560 divided by 40 = $14 per hour
Annie makes 950 divided by 40 = $23.75 per hour
Elise makes 375 divided by 40 = $9.38 per hour

Next, find out how many times their hourly wage goes into $125. This is the number of hours each needs to work to earn $125 for groceries.

Dylan must work (125 divided by 14) 8.9 hours
Annie must work (125 divided by 23.75) 5.3 hours
Elise must work (125/9.38) 13.3 hours

Chapter 3: College: Investing in Your Future
1) There are 52 weeks in a year. Multiply $471 × 52 to get the annual median earnings of someone with less than a high school diploma. Multiply 652 × 52 to get the annual median earnings of someone with a high school diploma, and so on for each of the educational levels.

Less than HS 471 × 52 = $24,492
HS Diploma 652 × 52 = $33,904
Some College 727 × 52 = $37,804
Associate Degree 785 × 52 = $40,820
Bachelor's Degree 1066 × 52 = $55,432
Master's Degree 1300 x 52 = $67,600
Professional Degree 1735 × 52 = $90,220
Doctoral Degree 1624 × 52 = $84,448

2) Multiply the median annual earnings of a worker with a high school diploma times 25 years. ($33,904 × 25 years = $847,600) Now do the same for a worker with a professional degree ($90,220 × 25 years = $2,255,500) Subtract the first from the second result to determine the difference between the two workers would earn over the course of twenty-five years (2,255,500–847,600 = $1,407,900).

Chapter 4: How Will I Pay for College?
Determine how much it would cost to attend each of the schools.

College #1
    $20,105 a year
    −$5,000 grant
    −$3,200 scholarship
    −$3,600 work study
    −$4,875 loan
  =$3,430 out of pocket expense

College #2
    $22,800 a year
    −$5,000 grant
    −$2,900 work study
    −$13,500 loans
  =$1,400 out of pocket expense

We know Jake has $3,000 of his own money plus $1,200 from his parents, for a total of $4,200 to spend.

While College #2 might be tempting because he would have less to pay up front, in the end, he would be much better off to choose College #1. He would have to borrow $8,625 more in student loans to attend college #2 for a year, and that's without factoring in the amount of interest he will have to pay.

Chapter 5: Understanding Income
1. A. $9 B. $0 (Until your earnings exceed $7,600 annually, you do not pay federal income taxes.) C. $25.92 D. $6.08 E. $32

2. To find out how much Thad earns annually including health care at his current job: Multiply his hourly wage of $18.50 × 40 hours a week= $740 × 52 weeks= $38,480 annual salary at his current job plus his health insurance cost of $600 per month × 12 months= $7,200 + $38,480 = $45,680. He is better off staying at his current job.

Chapter 6: Take It Further: Be an Entrepreneur
Jane will earn $8 an hour x 6 hours a week = $48 × 10 weeks = $480 baby-sitting on Tuesdays and Thursdays.

She will probably earn an additional $40 a weekend × 4 = $320, maybe more, maybe less depending on how often she works.

Jane will earn $200 × 4 weeks =$800 at the recreation program

She hopes to earn $200 to $400 at the yard sale. She will get $100 from watering plants and feeding fish for her friend's family.

$480 + $320 +$800 + $200 +$100 = $1,900

She is a little shy of her goal, but if she does well at the yard sale and takes on a few new baby-sitting jobs from her recreation job, she could easily reach it.

Index

Be Smart About Your Career